WORKBOOK

TRANSFORM YOUR INFORMATION
INTO ENTERTAINMENT AND YOUR
PODCAST INTO POWERFUL,
PROFITABLE RELATIONSHIPS

By ERIK K. JOHNSON
www.PodcastTalentCoach.com

CONTENTS

I.   Overview   p. 1

II.   Glossary   p. 7

III.   My Story   p. 9

IV.   Old World v. New World   p. 17

V.   Strategy   p. 23

VI.   Show Structure   p. 33

VII.   Your Voice   p. 41

VIII.   Preparation   p. 49

IX.   Topics   p. 55

X.   Tease & Promote   p. 61

XI.   Introductions   p. 65

XII.   Details   p. 71

XIII.   Topic Conclusions   p. 75

XIV.   Creative Writing   p. 79

XV.   Aircheck Info   p. 89

XVI.   Monetization   p. 101

XVII.   Conclusion   p. 111

XVIII.   Notes   p. 113

OVERVIEW

It is the podcast dream. You spend time each day or each week talking about your favorite subject. You record the talk and turn it into a podcast. Thousands and thousands of people find your podcast and listen religiously. The money comes rolling in, and your bank account fills up. You're a superstar!

Oh, if it were only that easy.

How do you make that money come rolling in? How do you fill your bank account using your podcast? How does that fantastic information in your brain actually convert to fantastic dollars in your pocket? How do you make the leap from attracting a large audience to attracting a healthy cashflow?

Those questions are the very reason this workbook is critical to your success. I will help you determine how to move your podcast beyond a simple transfer of information to become engaging entertainment. I will help you turn your podcast into a true, trusting relationship with your audience. I will then show you how to earn cash by leveraging that relationship, connection and trust.

There are four easy-to-understand steps to create winning podcasts. You will learn to find your passion. You will create a solid strategy based on a target and structure. You will fill your podcast with compelling, consistent content. Finally, you'll review each podcast methodically to make the next one even better. This workbook will help you take each of those steps.

The mistake most broke podcasters make is big and very common. It is a misconception of the large audience. A large audience doesn't necessarily equal a large bank account. An income generator needs to exist in order to generate a big bank account. Unless your audience is paying you to listen, which is incredibly rare, your audience is not the income generator.

Your income generator is your _relationship_ with your audience and the ways you leverage that relationship. It all begins by creating a very strong relationship. Your strong relationship begins with trust and takes time to develop.

When you create a solid relationship with your audience, you have tremendous power. You can use that relationship to motivate your audience to action. That action could be support of your sponsor or partner, purchase of your product or attendance at an event. That motivation to action can generate income. It can generate large sums of income in a hurry ... if you have first properly created the relationship.

This workbook will teach you how to create a trusting relationship with your audience. I will then teach you how to then leverage that relationship for income.

Your power begins with your relationship. If your relationship with your audience is similar to your relationship with the drive-thru attendant at the local burger joint that you see every other week but would not acknowledge at the ball game, you probably have very little power. On the other hand, if your relationship is similar to the relationship you have with your personal trainer that you see three times a week and with whom you swap birthday cards, you probably have tremendous power. You have built trust within the relationship with the personal trainer. If you make a recommendation to both indivuduals, the personal trainer is much more likely to follow your recommendation. If you hope to create money with your podcast, your relationship with your audience must be just as strong as your relationship with your personal trainer. You must work to build that trust.

To maintain trust with your audience, you must protect access to your audience with all you have. If the trust is broken, you will have a very difficult time generating any income. If you begin allowing access to your audience from other entities that do not have values identical to your values, people will no longer trust you.

If your audience feels you are only there to take without giving, you will build no trust. Give, give, give and give again before you ever hope to take. That is how you build trust. If your audience feels you are there to help them first, they can accept the fact that you are there to make money second. Getting the cart in front of the horse will get you nowhere fast.

Let's begin with the overview of your show. These questions will lay the foundation of your relationship.

WHAT IS YOUR STORY?

_____

_____

_____

_____

_____

_____

_____

HOW WILL YOU HELP PEOPLE?

_____

_____

_____

_____

_____

_____

_____

WHAT WILL YOU COMMUNICATE TO YOUR AUDIENCE?

_____

_____

_____

_____

_____

_____

_____

GLOSSARY

Before we begin, it will be helpful if we define a few terms.

Aircheck – The process of reviewing and critiquing the show. It is also shorthand for a copy of the show, i.e. "send me an aircheck of your show".

Co-host – A person on the show with equal stature as the host.

Demographic – The composition of a particular segment of the population.

Director – The person, usually not on the show, in charge of coordinating all elements and participants of the show.

Host – The individual on the show in charge of leading the show.

Podcast – A series of multimedia files, usually audio or video episodes, made available on the internet for subscription and download through syndication or streaming.

Producer – The person behind the scenes of the show who helps set up the content, such as interviews, audio clips, visual aids or guests.

Program Director – Individual in charge of all on-air elements of a radio staton.

Show Prep – The preparation of the show content prior to the beginning of the show.

Sidekick – The person on the show, lower in stature than the host, with a supporting role.

Target Audience – The desired audience the show is designed to attract, though not the only audience the show will attract.

MY STORY

I struggled long and hard to develop a trusting relationship with my audience over my 25-year career in radio. I learned the hard way. Let my lumps and bumps help you avoid the typical pitfalls.

My first job on the radio was a part-time position running longform programming on a very, very small AM station. My responsibility simply involved introducing the programs and providing the time and temperature. After providing that thirty seconds of information, I would play the show while sitting around for about thirty minutes. There was very little relationship involved.

When I got my first show on a music station, I acted like I thought every radio announcer acted. It was still part-time, but I was on the radio. I used all the radio cliches. I had the cheesy radio voice. The show was painful. The ratings were just as painful. There was no relationship.

Over time, I began to be myself. My show and content was authentic. My topics were centered around my interests. I began to reveal things about myself, and over time, I built a trusting relationship with my audience. The relationship philosophy finally clicked for me, and I have been near the top ever since.

I have also coached many others to do the same with even greater success. I launched a station and took it to the top of the ratings in one year. After programming that station for ten years, I became the Program Director of a heritage station in the market. That station has also been near the top of the ratings for over four years. By spreading the relationship philosophy, both station became quite successful.

It took me many years to learn and refine my relationship approach to broadcasting. It is the product of hours and hours of listening to great shows by others. I learned from mentors, seminars, books and mistakes. I now use this system to help talent create powerful relationships with their audience. It will help you as well.

My talent coaching career began in 1995. It started with stereotypes. I had my talent doing typical call-in topics that we thought might generate some phone calls to our radio shows. We were doing radio gags that we thought people might find funny. Unfortunately, the material was stale and didn't generate much interest.

Over the years, I began to refine my own show. I began to be myself by first dropping the radio stage name. The topics of discussion on my show were primarily of interest to me. I began doing things I found entertaining. The more I followed this path, the more the audience reacted.

The ratings for my show began to increase the more I was authentic on the air. In public, people would mention personal things I had done on the air. Fans wouldn't mention the funny bit I did. They would mention the personal anecdote I mentioned in passing. The more I behaved like their friend, the more they responded like a friend. I built a ratings success by being myself.

I began introducing the relationship method to other talent on my staff. It was difficult for them to begin to move away from the stereotypical radio show and move toward the material they actually found interesting. Most radio hosts don't believe they should entertain themselves. They are being paid to entertain others. It was a slow introduction to the system.

My on-air personalities began to realize the power of the relationship method. They slowly began to introduce the systen into their shows. They would reveal a small thing about themselves on the air. This would usually occur while they were discussing some other typical radio bit. The audience would react to the personal piece without hardly mentioning the traditional "topic". The light started to go off.

These radio people were stunned that they could actually discuss the things that were of interest to them. For so long, they have been working under the impression and direction that they needed to tailor their on-air material specifically for their audience. They simply didn't realize that their interests are also the interests of their audience.

The relationship method eventually became the primary system for the shows. The on-air talent spent most of the show discussing topics that piqued their interest. In turn, the topics also attracted the audience. The shows went to the top of the ratings by attracting large audiences.

These questions will help you define the primary topic and focus of your show.

WHAT ARE YOU PASSIONATE ABOUT?

_____

_____

_____

_____

_____

WHAT ARE YOUR UNIQUE QUALITIES?

_____

_____

_____

_____

_____

_____

_____

WHAT TOPIC TENDS TO OCCUPY MOST OF YOUR CONVERSATIONS?

_____

_____

_____

_____

_____

_____

_____

WHAT DO YOU LIKE TO DO IN YOUR SPARE TIME?

_____

_____

_____

_____

_____

_____

_____

OLD WORLD V. NEW WORLD

It's a new world out there. I'm not talking about the transformation from radio to podcast. I'm talking about the transformation from the theater to the broadcast. Before we dive into the the nuts and bolts of your show, let's look at the stage.

Before there was the podcast, there was the television. Before the television, there was the radio. Before radio was introduced to the public, people were entertained by attending stage performances as a group. People would gather at the theater to be entertained by a performer or group of performers. The audience would sit attentively while the performer entertained. The individual on stage would address the crowd. The crowd would react. It was typically a one-way dialog with one addressing many.

Radio came along as the new form of entertainment. Here was a wonderful device that could reach many households at once. Broadcasters had a problem. They needed material to broadcast.

They turned to the theater. Early broadcasts were simply transmissions of the events taking place at the theater. Radio would broadcast concerts, comedy routines, drama performances and the like.

Radio started with an individual onstage addressing a large crowd. They would say something like, "Ladies and Gentlemen, good evening!" It was one individual addressing a crowd in a theater that was then broadcast over the airwaves. The radio audience was simply eavesdropping on the performance.

Over the years, radio evolved, but the radio talent did not. Radio is now one-on-one. However, the hosts on the radio continue to treat the "audience" as a group in a theater rather than as an individual in a conversation.

It is a new broadcast world. Podcasting is the new broadcasting frontier. As a podcaster, you can capitalize on the relationship method and turn your podcast into money.

Just like radio, your podcast is an intimate conversation. The conversation is usually one person speaking into a microphone addressing a single individual. There may sometimes be hundreds of thousands of people listening. However, they are all listening by themselves. Even in an automobile with others over communal speakers, the members of the audience are listening by themselves in their own head.

Just like radio, your podcast is a personal medium. Most people use radio as a companion. Even when the radio is on in the background, people have it turned on so they don't feel alone. Rarely will someone drive in the car without something playing on the stereo unless they are on the phone. Some get comfort in their favorite CDs. Others like the mental conversation they have with the on-air talent. We are a communal creature. As humans, we love interaction with others. We love to create community. Hearing others speak to us through our radio helps create community.

Even as we create community, people listen individually. Audio isn't like television. Audio is unique to each imagination.

When a story is viewed on television, everyone watching that show is seeing the same thing. When you watch tv, you know what the characters are wearing. You know if the sky is cloudy. You know if other characters are present in the scene.

When someone tells a story, on the radio or in a podcast, it is theater of the mind. When you hear a story, the scenery is playing out in your mind in a unique way unlike the way anyone else could envision it. No other person is imagining the clothing of the characters the exact same way you are imagining them. That theater is unique to you. You are listening and imagining by yourself.

Podcasts make the one-on-one approach even more important. Podcasts are often enjoyed through headphones. Your audience is truly listening by themselves. The headphones block out all other sounds and distractions.   You have multiple "one person" audiences at the same time. Yet, it is still one person.

Create a great theater.   The theater will be different for each listener, because they are using their individual imagination. Create a movie and put the listener in it.   Make the story an individual experience for the listener.   Engage the listener with vivid details and a fantastic storyline. Make them forget they are listening to a podcast.

Create great theater of the mind.

STRATEGY

As you create your podcast, you need to determine a strategy for the show. You need to have focus. You need to find that one thing that will make you the expert that rises above the rest. When you pair that focus with the structure for the show, you will have your strategy. Your strategy will be your angle.

Your strategy will help you become memorable. If you create it correctly, your strategy will make you stand out. To get noticed, you must make your show unique. Be bold, take chances and stand for something. Be different. When you are different, you stand out and people will remember you.

WHAT MAKES YOU UNIQUE?

_____

_____

_____

_____

_____

_____

_____

WHAT WILL YOU STAND FOR?

_____

_____

_____

_____

_____

_____

_____

WHAT WILL MAKE PEOPLE REMEMBER YOU?

_____

_____

_____

_____

_____

_____

_____

You are creating a brand with your podcast. Great brands consistently communicate one message. Think of the best known brands. The best soda is defined by the real thing. Serving more hamburgers than anyone in the world. Save 15% on your car insurance. You're a great athlete ... just do it! Coca Cola, McDonalds, Geico, and Nike. They all deliver consistent messages and thereby become solid brands.

Before you create your strategy, you need to define your target audience. You will approach fans of the Oakland Raiders of the National Football League different than you would talk to fans of the New York Philharmonic. You will speak differently to young men in college than you would to grandmothers who enjoy knitting. When you define your target audience, you will define your strategy to reach that audience.

If you are creating a podcast around retirement, your target audience may be defined by gender and age, such as men in their early twenties or 50-year-old women. Their age is the commonality.

Your target audience could also be defined by a common passion. The podcast could cater to fans of Harley Davidson who ride at least 25,000 miles per year. Their fanatacism ties them together.

Let's create your ideal listener. The more you know, the better you will be able to communicate.

WHAT IS THE GENDER OF YOUR IDEAL LISTENER?

_____

WHAT IS THE AGE OF YOUR IDEAL LISTENER?

_____

WHAT IS THEIR MARITAL STATUS?

_____

DESCRIBE THEIR FAMILY?

_____

_____

_____

_____

_____

_____

_____

WHAT LEVEL OF SCHOOLING HAVE THEY COMPLETED?

_____

WHAT TYPE OF JOB DO THEY HAVE?

_____

_____

WHAT IS THEIR INCOME LEVEL?

_____

WHAT KIND OF CAR DO THEY DRIVE?

_____

WHAT MAGAZINES DO THEY READ?

_____

_____

_____

_____

WHAT TV SHOWS DO THEY WATCH?

_____

_____

_____

_____

TO WHAT OTHER PODCASTS DO THEY LISTEN?

_____

_____

_____

_____

_____

HOW OFTEN DO THEY LISTEN TO PODCATS?

_____

_____

_____

WHO ARE THEIR HEROES?

_____

_____

_____

_____

_____

_____

_____

WHAT IS THEIR GREATEST WANT?

_____

_____

_____

_____

_____

_____

_____

WHAT IS THEIR GREATEST NEED?

_____

_____

_____

_____

_____

_____

_____

WHAT IS THEIR GREATEST FEAR?

_____

_____

_____

_____

_____

_____

_____

WHAT PROBLEM DO THEY NEED SOLVED?

_____

_____

_____

_____

_____

_____

_____

SHOW STRUCTURE

Structure is necessary to build consistency and trust with your fans. The audience expects specific elements each time they listen to your show. They expect your style to be consistent. Your audience expects the host to be the same for each show. You must deliver to that expectation to build the trust with your fans. This trust is where podcast monetization begins.

The structure of your show is defined by the Five "Ws". Develop the structure of your show by determining Who, What, When, Where and Why. While the structure will be the same for every show, the content will vary within this structure.

As you create your show structure and define the "Who", there are various roles that are possible. Here are few potential roles on any given show.

Generator – This is the individual who launches the question, topic or lead into the material to be discussed.

Reactor – This is the individual on the show who reacts to the content served up by the generator.

Director - The person, usually not on the show, in charge of coordinating all elements and participants of the show.

Producer - The person behind the scenes of the show who helps set up the content, such as interviews, audio clips, visual aids or guests.

Co-hosts or host/sidekick – Co-hosts are two equal hosts on the show. The host/sidekick relationship is one defined by a leader (host) and a supporter (sidekick).

Let's develop the structure of your show.

WHO WILL THE AUDIENCE HEAR ON THE SHOW?

SINGLE INDIVIDUAL? CO-HOSTS? HOST AND SIDEKICK?

INTERVIEWS? CALLERS?

_____

_____

_____

_____

_____

_____

HOW WILL THE DIFFERENT VOICE CONTRAST AND

COMPLIMENT EACH OTHER?

_____

_____

_____

_____

_____

_____

_____

WHAT WILL BE ON YOUR SHOW? THIS INCLUDES
TOPICS, INTERVIEWS, CALLERS, E-MAIL, AUDIO CLIPS,
HIGHLIGHTS, SOUND BITES, ARTICLES AND OTHER
MATERIAL YOU MIGHT INCLUDE IN YOUR CONTENT.
FIND THE "WHAT" THAT EXCITES YOU.

_____

_____

_____

_____

_____

_____

_____

WHEN WILL YOU RECORD AND POST YOUR SHOW? FIND
THE TIME OF DAY WHEN YOU HAVE THE MOST ENERGY
TO RECORD YOUR SHOW.

_____

_____

YOU ALSO NEED TO DECIDE HOW OFTEN YOU WILL
CREATE A SHOW. YOUR FANS NEED TO TRUST THAT THE
SHOW WILL BE THERE WHEN YOU SAY IT WILL BE
THERE. SELECT A SCHEDULE THAT YOU CAN HANDLE
ON A CONSISTENT BASIS.

_____

_____

_____

WHERE WILL YOU CREATE YOUR SHOW? THIS IS AN IMPORTANT DETAIL. EACH EPISODE OF YOUR SHOW COULD COME FROM YOUR "STUDIO". YOU COULD RECORD YOUR SHOW ON LOCATION IF YOU ARE INCORPORATING GUESTS. THE TECHNOLOGY AVAILABLE TODAY WILL ALLOW YOU TO RECORD ALMOST ANYWHERE. FIND A PLACE WHERE YOU CAN FOCUS ON YOUR SHOW AND CONTROL THE SURROUNDING AMBIENT NOISE. LOCATION IS AN IMPORTANT FACTOR TO THE PROFESSIONAL SOUND OF YOUR SHOW.

_____

_____

_____

_____

_____

_____

_____

WHY ARE YOU CREATING A PODCAST? YOU NEED TO
FIND YOUR PASSION. IF YOU ARE CREATING A PODCAST
FOR REASONS OTHER THAN YOUR PASSIONS, YOU WILL
FIND IT DIFFICULT TO KEEP UP THE CONSISTENCY
REQUIRED TO BE SUCCESSFUL.

_____

_____

_____

_____

_____

_____

_____

YOUR VOICE

Here are just a few thoughts to make your voice stronger.

Warm up for about ten minutes before recording. To properly warm up, start at a natural tone and slowly expand your range to the extremes over the next five minutes. This will make your voice stronger and help it last longer. Proper warm-up is critical for the health of your vocal chords.

Drink water. Avoid soda and similar drinks. They coat the thoat and negatively affect the vocal chords. Your water should also be room temperature. Cold water contracts the vocal chords.

Stand while you record if possible. Speak from the diaphram and talk at a slight, upward angle. Standing opens your chest and throat. Your voice will have a full sound if you are speaking from your diaphram while standing.

Relax and smile. If you are tense, your audience will notice. They will also be able to hear your smile come through the speakers. It may sound crazy. If you want to test the theory, record the same line twice. Record it once while smiling and once while not smiling. Then, listen to the recording. Believe me ... you'll hear the difference.

Use a natural voice and don't yell. Your audience will notice if you are trying to talk in a tone lower than your natural voice. Be comfortable, and be yourself.

"I hate the way I sound."

I hear that complaint quite often. Many people do not like the sound of their own voice. It is quite common.

It is also quite natural to dislike the sound of you own voice when hearing a recorded version of it. When you talk, the bones in your head vibrate adding to the qualities you naturally hear. When you hear a recording of your voice, those vibrations are absent causing your voice to sound different to you.

The natural bone vibrations also make you do some unnecessary acrobatics with your voice when using headphones. The bone vibrations combined with the enclosed nature of your headphones cause you to hear the big announcer voice in a much different way the listener hears it. You tend to speak in ways you don't normally speak in everyday conversation.

There are six steps you can take to make your voice sound more natural and get you on the path to enjoying the sound of your voice.

1. Notes, not script

The structure you use when you write is much different than the structure you use when you speak. You use different words. Your sentence structure will be different. The flow of the written word simply differs greatly from the spoken word.

As you are speaking, use notes instead of a full script. You will sound much more comfortable when speaking from the heart rather than speaking from the script. The flow and structure of your sentences will be much more natural.

Make note of the important points to include in your podcast. Hit those points within your show without reading it word for word.

2. Talk to one person

You will sound much more natural when you speak to one person rather than a group of people. When I am listening to your podcast, I want to feel like you are talking to me. If you include a call to action in your podcast, you want me to act upon that request. If you are talking to a group of people, I can easily think someone else will take action and I can do nothing.

If you are speaking directly to me, we will begin to develop a friendship. I will begin to feel like I know you. I will also feel like you care about me personally. Your delivery will sound much more conversational and less like a lecture when you speak to one person. This will help you become more comfortable with your own voice.

3. One ear headphone

Your voice will sound different to you when you listen to your voice through headphones. The enclosed space of the headphones ampliphies your voice. The sound of your voice is also changed by the audio processing. The bones in your head vibrate differently when using headphones.

To help you sound more natural, remove one ear of your headphones. With only one cup on your ear, you are able to hear your voice more naturally with the free ear. You will also hear your voice in the context of the ambient room noise rather than through the vacuum of the headphones.

4. Turn your headphones down

If you are wearing only one cup of your headphones, turning the volume down will also help you sound more natural. With a lower headphone volume, you will better hear your natural voice. You won't be fooled by the dominance of the headphone sound.

Use your headphones to make sure you hear the other audio included in your podcast. Make sure you can hear your music bed, intro, guest and other audio. However, make sure your headphones are not giving you a false image of your voice.

5. Don't get sing-songy

Speak naturally. Do not attempt to sound like other announcers you have heard. Be yourself.

When you speak like an announcer, you begin to strech and emphasize words unnaturally. Your speech begins to unnaturally bounce. When you listen to your recorded voice, you may sound like a puky disc jockey or used car salesman on a bad television commercial. Both lack warmth. They are hard to believe. You will sound less natural with you use the announcer voice.

Speak conversationally. Use a natural pace. Don't use unnecessary emphasis on words. Speak as if you are on the telephone. These steps will help your voice sound more natural.

6. Review your show

The best way to become a more natural speaker is to review your show often.

When you listen to your show on a regular basis, you will become much more accustomed to hearing your voice in a recorded setting. You dislike your voice, because you are not used to hearing it outside of your own head. The more you hear your voice, the more natural it will sound.

It is possible to overcome the dislike of your own voice. You simply have to take steps to conquer it. It will take time to begin liking the sound of your voice. Be patient.

Remove some of the annoying qualities of your speech. Use notes, speak to one person and get rid of the sing-songy pattern. Polish up the product first.

Next, adjust the way your record. Use only one cup of your headphones. Turn the volume down a bit to hear your voice in its natural setting.   Make minor adjustments until you get comfortable.

Finally, review your show. When listening to your own voice becomes habit, your recorded voice will sound much more natural to you. Review your show often.

PREPARATION

Now that you have developed your strategy and stucture, it is time to load your show with great content. This is where the relationship is built. Your content will deliver the personal touch that will build trust between you and your fans. This is where you shine.

Content is King. In order to develop great content, you must prepare. On the radio, many great hosts use the rule of thumb of two hours of preparation for every hour they are on the air. It is not as easy as opening the microphone and rambling for 30 minutes. You need to know how to structure your content segments and what you hope to accomplish with that content. Content is king and should be treated as such with proper preparation.

Just like the Boy Scouts say ... Be Prepared. When you are prepared, you earn credibility.

There is no reason for you to start down the path of a topic without being prepared. It is up to you to plan what is coming and what details you need. Prepare and prepare a little more.

Many hosts open the mic and wing it. Now, I don't mean to imply they just say whatever comes to mind. However, I do mean to say that they select a topic or two, or maybe a few e-mails to answer. They come up with an angle on a superficial level and run with it without doing their homework. I hear quite a few shows where the talent won't have the stats at hand, the proper pronounciation of a name, or even the address of a website they mention. There is no excuse for being unprepared like that.

The most important question to ask is, "Why is it on the show?" You should be able to answer this question for everything you do. If it doesn't have a great reason, like engaging the audience or motivating them to buy or fostering the relationship, it shouldn't be on the show. These questions will help you determine why any topic is on the show.

Let's develop a show prep plan for your podcast.

WHAT ARE THE INTERESTING TOPICS YOU HOPE TO
ADDRESS ON THIS PARTICULAR EPISODE?

_____

_____

_____

_____

_____

WHAT DO YOU HOPE TO ACCOMPLISH WITH BOTH THE
TOPIC AND THE SHOW OVERALL?

_____

_____

_____

_____

_____

HOW WILL YOU TREAT EACH SPECIFIC TOPIC YOU HOPE TO ADDRESS? WHAT WILL YOU DO WITH THE CONTENT? (Answer the question, demonstrate the answer, play some audio, show charts to support your answer, etc.)

_____

_____

_____

_____

_____

CREATE AN OUTLINE FOR THE FLOW OF THE SHOW TOPICS. (This is important for the show introduction.)

_____

_____

_____

_____

_____

WHAT SUPPORTING INFORMATION WILL YOU NEED FOR

THE SHOW? (Organize and highlight for easy access during the

show.)

_____

_____

_____

_____

_____

_____

_____

TOPICS

To be memorable, there are a few questions you need to ask. Just like our five "Ws" helped shape the structure of the show, these questions will help shape the content of the show. These questions should be asked for every show and every individual topic. They will shape your material into memorable content.

What do you want the listener to feel? Just as numbers make your audience lose interest, emotions get your audience engaged. An emotional connection will suck them into the show. Create a relationship and emotional bond with your listeners to create trust, loyalty and frequent engagement. Find their deepest wants, needs & fears and begin at that point. When you stir strong emotions within your listeners, you are on the path to creating long-term, passionate fans.

There are many emotions that you could stir in your listener. These include anger, fear, annoyance, doubt, envy, frustration, sadness, shock, amusement, delight, excitement, affection, empathy, courage, hope, relaxation or surprise. These are just a few. There are many others. You can also elicit multiple emotions with the same story. For example, a charity story could stir both empathy and optimism simultaneously.

Friendship comes from self-revelation. Friendship is where trust and loyalty begin. This is how great brands are created. It is a long journey of many steps. Each self-revelation you make as part of your show is another step in that journey. Over time, you move beyond awareness to simple acquaintance to familiar colleague to lifelong friend. Your self-revelations will stir emotions in your listeners and be the building blocks of your friendship.

Here is the worksheet for each topic on the show.

WHY IS THE TOPIC RELEVANT TO YOUR AUDIENCE?

_____

_____

_____

HOW WILL YOU MAKE THE AUDIENCE CARE?

_____

_____

_____

WHAT IS THE SOURCE OF THE TOPIC?

_____

_____

_____

HOW WILL THE SOURCE LEND CREDIBILITY TO THE TOPIC?

_____

_____

_____

_____

WHAT DO YOU FIND INTRIGUING ABOUT THE TOPIC?

_____

_____

_____

_____

WHAT EMOTION DO YOU HOPE TO STIR?

_____

_____

_____

_____

IN WHAT CONTEXT WILL THE STORY BE SET?

_____

_____

_____

WHERE WILL YOU TAKE THE TOPIC? WHERE WILL THE
STORY GO?

_____

_____

_____

_____

WHAT DETAILS WILL YOU USE?

_____

_____

_____

_____

WHAT IS THE ONE THING YOU HOPE YOUR LISTENER
WILL REMEMBER ABOUT LISTENING TO YOU?

_____

_____

_____

_____

WRITE THE INTRIGUING INTRODUCTION TO YOUR TOPIC.

_____

_____

_____

_____

_____

_____

_____

TEASE & PROMOTE

Teasing is the art of creating anticipation for your audience to entice them to stick around for the payoff to your setup. It is a critical element of your show. Teasing helps create the momentum of the show.

When you promote parts of the show that are coming up, you must creatively tease your audience. You must give them a reason to stick around. The evening news does a wonderful job at teasing.

The trick to a creative tease is not only what you tell your audience. A successful tease is highly dependent on what you leave out of the story during the tease. Give the audience 80% of the story, but leave out the punch line. "There is something in the school lunch that is causing the grades of students to drop. Find out how your child can avoid it tonight on the 10 o'clock news." That is a solid tease for the news. You need to do that with your stories.

If you have an interview later in your show, tease it creatively. "John Smith will join us on the show to describe the method he used to generate $100,000 in sales in just 30 days with online marketing." Make them want to stick around.

WRITE A CREATIVE TEASE FOR THIS STORY:

Up to a dozen tornadoes skipped through the densely populated Dallas-Fort Worth area in Texas on Tuesday, ripping apart homes, tossing tractor-trailer trucks into the air and injuring at least 17 people, but there were no reported deaths. Ten to 12 tornadoes touched down during a massive storm that brought chaos from high winds, rain and hail to the nation's fourth most populous metropolitan area, said National Weather Service meteorologist Jesse Moore. On Wednesday morning, more than 8,000 homes and business were still without electricity. Many of the 6.3 million area residents were forced to scramble for safety Tuesday as the storm bore down during the early afternoon, when schools and workplaces were open. Seven people were injured in the suburb of Arlington, police said. Most suffered only minor injuries but one person hit by a falling tree was in critical condition, said Arlington

police spokeswoman Cheryl Carpenter.

_____

_____

_____

_____

_____

_____

_____

_____

_____

_____

_____

_____

_____

_____

INTRODUCTIONS

Once you have teased the audience, you will eventually reach the point where you tell the story. Great storytellers structure their stories just like great speeches. Use an intriguing introduction, vivid details and a powerful conclusion. Those are the three elements to every great story.

The first thing we learned in speech class was the structure of a speech. The good speech is built with an introduction, a body and a conclusion. Your podcast is no different. However, it may be structured like a series of tiny speeches. But, let's not get ahead of ourselves.

Your introduction should set up your podcast. It should be an intriguing introduction that tells the listener exactly what the podcast is all about. What will I get when I listen? It doesn't matter whether your podcast is 10 minutes or 60 minutes long. You need to tell the listener what is to come.

"Welcome to the Podcast Talent Coach podcast. My name is Erik K. Johnson. Over the next 30 minutes, I will help you transform your information into engaging entertainment and your podcast into powerful, profitable relationships."

With that quick introduction, I told you exactly what to expect. You know the name of my podcast. You know the name of the host. You know exactly how long my podcast will run. You know the goal we are setting out to accomplish. I've also put you in the mix by referencing your dreams and how my podcast will help you. In those brief seconds, I've given you who, what, when and why.

Your introduction must be intriguing. This is true for the overall podcast introduction and the introduction to your stories. "Today we are going to talk about work" is not intriguing. That will not make anyone want to stick around to hear what you have to say, especially for 30 minutes or an hour. "Today we are going to answer four e-mails to help these individuals escape their dreaded

9-to-5 and get into their dream jobs." That is a statement that will stir some emotion and make people listen through to the end.

It is critical that you tell the listener what your podcast is all about EVERY time. Your show will have new listeners with every episode. You cannot assume they heard the first podcast, or even one of the first twenty-five. Each time you begin a podcast, you have to assume someone is hearing your show for the first time. Even those that have been listening since the beginning will find comfort hearing that consistent opening they can almost recite verbatim. They'll feel like they are in the club, while the new listeners will now be up to speed.

Remember, it is everytime.

Failing to introduce everytime is the one misstep I hear most often with podcasts. Talent get too comfortable with their podcast after doing it ten or twenty times. The podcast gets lucky enough to make it into the top ten. People discover it, and the podcast begins with no introduction as if the listener stepped into the middle of a conversation. It becomes uncomfortable for the new listeners. The podcast suddenly stops growing its audience. Remember, your show will always be new to somebody.

You will have new listeners every time you post a new podcast. You cannot assume your audience has heard your podcast before. You need to set up the show at the beginning to let the new audience members know what they can expect while letting the returning fans feel comfortable without being bored.

WHAT DO YOU HOPE TO MAKE THE LISTENER FEEL WITH THIS STORY?

_____

_____

_____

_____

_____

HOW WILL YOU ENGAGE THE LISTENER WITH YOUR INTRODUCTION?

_____

_____

_____

_____

_____

_____

_____

WHAT WILL YOUR POSITION BE FOR THE STORY?

_____

_____

_____

_____

_____

_____

DETAILS

The next step for your story is the descriptive details. The details make your story magical. If you make sure your details are powerful, your story will be memorable.

When someone tells a story, on the radio or in a podcast, it is theater of the mind. When you hear the old time radio show describe the dim light on in the servants' quarters, the scenery is playing out in your mind in a unique way unlike the way anyone else could envision it. No other person is imagining the clothing of the characters the exact same way you are imagining them. That mental theater is unique to you. You are listening and imagining by yourself.

Podcasts make the one-on-one approach even more important. Podcasts are often enjoyed through headphones. Your audience is truly listening by themselves. The headphones block out all other sounds and distractions. Your podcast will have multiple "one person" audiences at the same time. Yet, it is still one person.

Connect with your "one person" audience by creating a great theater. The theater will be different for each listener, because they are using their individual imagination. Create a movie and put the listener in it. Make the story an individual experience for the listener. Engage the listener with vivid details and a fantastic storyline. Make them forget they are listening to a podcast. Create great theater of the mind. Create unique, vivid, mental images.

Your details should contain active language. Words like walking, carrying, and eating are current tense. They create images in your mind. You can see a clown walking. If I am telling a story about a clown that walked, using the past tense, it is more difficult to envision in your mind. It already happened. He isn't doing it anymore. I can see walking. I can't see walked.

When you use active language, your story comes to life. Use rich, vivid words that will draw fantastic pictures in the minds of your audience. "The old man, small and fragile, came slowly walking into the art shop gingerly carrying the tattered, leather-bound, black-and-white photo album he had been saving from his depression-era childhood." You can see the old man. Active language paints those photos.

Create theater of the mind.

The use of active language will stir the imagination of your listener and help you connect to your audience. Put the listener in the moment. Make the listener see the action you are describing.

"I'm walking in the bustling restaurant and shaking off the cold without even watching where I'm walking." That is active language. In your mind, you can see me walking in.

Sure, your restaurant may be different from my restaurant. That difference is what makes theater of the mind great. You see it the way you think it fits best for you. Your scene doesn't need to match my scene in order for the story to make sense. It is your theater.

Active language connects each listener to the story in his or her own way. It will create strong audience engagement. Active language during storytelling is a powerful tool you can use while you're building your podcast.

Make your words vivid. Sell the sizzle of the story. This will put your listener right in the middle of the story. Make it come to life.

Create a great podcast brand. Create theater of the mind.

TOPIC CONCLUSION

Your conclusion should be just as powerful as your introduction. Leave your audience with a bang. Make them remember the story.

When you are discussing a topic, take the first opportunity to get out of the bit. You will keep your audience engaged. You will maintain the momentum of the show. You will also avoid repeating yourself and becoming boring. Take the first exit.

There are clues in your show that let you know you've missed the opportunity to end the bit. When you find yourself saying things like "as I said", "like I was saying", or "as we've discussed", you have missed your exit. Those phrases are simply additional ways to say, "let me repeat this again". Once you have reached that point, you are stating your introduction point again. This should be your conclusion. Move on to the next discussion.

If you miss the exit, you begin retracing your steps. You begin offering information you've already provided. Your listener then begins thinking of other things, because they have heard this part before. I got it. Let's move on.

Only you will know when you have offered enough information to make your point. Once you have made your point, keep the show moving. Move onto the next topic. Keep your audience engaged.

Plan your exit before you begin. Know how you will get out of the topic before you start. If you know where you are going, it is much easier to get there. It is also easier to recognize when you have arrived. Develop a powerful conclusion before the topic begins. Then, take the first exit.

How will you get out of the story? Write your conclusion.

_____

_____

_____

_____

_____

_____

_____

_____

_____

_____

_____

CREATIVE WRITING

TELL YOUR STORY THREE DIFFERENT WAYS

The key to a consistent and entertaining podcast is to be able to communicate the main points of your strategy in different ways. You need to be able to tell the same story using different words.

Podcasters are always looking for new things to talk about on their show. They want to keep their content fresh. Podcasters are concerned their content will get stale if they keep repeating the same message episode after episode.

It is understandable that podcasters want to continue to deliver new content. You want to keep your listeners returning for new ideas. When you are delivering the same message over and over, there is potential for your content to get boring and stale. However, when you stray too far from the core message, you run the risk of diluting your brand.

There was a time when I would enjoy a particular podcast about business and marketing. I would listen to it on a regular basis. This went on for a few months until they drove me to unsubscribe.

I began noticing the show would post inconsistently. Sometimes it would be weekly. Other times a new episode wouldn't show up for a month. I never knew what to expect.

The show was hosted by two people in different locations. During some episodes they would talk about hiking. There were times they would discuss the weather differences between the two cities. Many times the discussions were not at all pertinent to the topic of business or marketing.

The hosts would also answer all sorts of questions, regardless of topic relevance. It sounded as if they answered every e-mail they received. There was such a variety of topics that I sometimes wondered if they changed the focus of the show.

I had come to this show to learn something about business and marketing. The show looked like it might have some information I could use in my business. Unfortunately, it seldom delivered on the promise of the show brand. The show was too inconsistent.

Eventually, I unsubscribed.

There are hundreds of podcasts about business and marketing. If you want to stand out from the crowd, you need to be unique, be the best, be exciting, and be consistent.

Frequency to the target is the way to get your audience to remember your show and marketing message. So, how can you be unique and consistent at the same time? How do you deliver a consistent message without getting boring or stale? How can you keep your content fresh while delivering the information your audience expects from your show?

There are five ways to deliver a consistent message with your podcast without getting stale.

1. Say the same things with different words.

Find different ways to package your message. Keep the brand message consistent. Simply find new ways to illustrate your point.

On The Dave Ramsey Show, Dave teaches his seven baby steps to get out of debt and build wealth. His entire show is based around those seven steps. Nearly every call and question comes back to one of those steps. He has built an empire and 20-year radio show around seven steps. It's the same thing on every show. Dave simply finds new ways to illustrate the method. It is a consistent message. He uses different ways to say it.

When looking for new ways to frame your brand message, you could approach the subject in many ways. It could be from your point of view or the listeners point of view. It could be in relation to the elderly or young. You could describe it through the eyes of somebody from another country or somebody that speaks a different language. How would the rich and poor see it differently? Describe how a beginner might use your information. Then, describe it from the standpoint of a professional. Those are ten different ways to communicate the same message using different words.

2. Give it context.

Dan O'Day is one of my mentors. I have attended many of his seminars and purchased quite a few of his products. He teaches broadcasters how to craft their sales message.

In one of his presentations, Dan gave a fantastic example of context. Dan asked, "Is it wrong to take medication from a co-worker's desk?" How would you answer that question?

Then, Dan gave the question some context.

What if someone in your office was having a heart attack and that medication was the only thing that could save them?

That is the definition of context. On the surface, sure, taking medicine is wrong. Give the story some context, and you might just change your mind.

3. Decide on the perspective for the story.

What is your position on the subject? Take a stand. If you don't care enough to be on one side or the other, how can you expect your audience to pick a side and care?

What do you hope to communicate with this topic? What is the one thing you want your audience to remember about this episode? Answer those two questions and you will begin to define your perspective.

Pick an angle that will really make the story stand out. If you are discussing hunger in Africa, you could tell the story from the point of view of an energetic volunteer, a hopeless child experiencing it firsthand, a frustrated government worker fighting the bureaucracy, or an immigrant to this country who has discovered new hope. Different perspectives communicate different messages.

4. Communicate with passion.

Love what you do. It is much easier to find different ways to say the same thing when you love what you do. Be passionate about a topic, and you'll be able to talk about it all day long.

Excitement and passion are contagious. If you are excited about your topic, your listener will be engaged and excited as well. Have you ever met that person that was so excited to talk about a subject that you found yourself getting sucked into a conversation that wouldn't have had any interest to you at any other time? Thirty minutes later you realize you're still talking about the same subject.

Make your listener love you or hate you. Either way you are making them care. The middle is boring. Nobody has ever said, "Wow, did you hear the show today? He really had no opinion one way or the other." Push people to pick a side. You will make them emotionally vested in your show.

5. Sell the sizzle.

Consumers do not buy products. They buy product benefits. People do not want products and services. They want to solve their problems. What problem will your product or service solve?

People will buy the results and benefits of your product or service.

Be consistent with your benefit message. Find different ways to deliver the message of your benefit in different ways. We are transforming your information into engaging entertainment. Information sounds like a boring message. Let's juice up your content and make it engaging. Sell the sizzle.

List ten ways to introduce yourself. (On the phone, at a party, to
an old friend, etc.)

_____

_____

_____

_____

_____

_____

_____

_____

_____

_____

Tell a brief story of how you met your childhood friend in three different ways.

_____

_____

_____

_____

_____

_____

_____

_____

_____

_____

_____

_____

_____

_____

_____

AIRCHECK INFO

Reviewing your show is critical to your success. If you don't analyze your show and figure out how to improve it, your show will never get better. In radio, the critique of a show is called an aircheck.

To successfully critique your show, you need to know where to look to see what worked and what can be improved. These points will help you see if you've accomplished all the things we've developed up to this point.

If you have followed the steps in the prep stage, you defined your goals for your show before you began. You know where you wanted to take the show and what you hoped to accomplish. Now it is time to see if that actually happened.

Do not see it as a failure if you didn't follow your plan exactly. There are times when opportunities for better material arise. The trick is to know when to use the new opportunity in place of the old material. That knowledge will come with time and with the more shows you record. As you review your podcast, do not simply judge it on whether or not you stuck to the script. You need to judge your show by the acomplishment of the goals you've established.

Grab your goal sheet as you prepare to answer the following questions. We will dig through the show to see what worked. Finding the successful points is just as important as what did not work and needs to be fixed. Adding great content that works will be a key ingredient to the success of the show. Find those "oh wow" moments.

Answer the following questions as you listen to your full podcast.

WHAT DID YOU HOPE TO ACCOMPLISH ON THIS SHOW?

DID YOU SUCCEED?

_____

_____

_____

_____

_____

HOW DID YOU MAKE THE AUDIENCE CARE?

_____

_____

_____

_____

WHERE WERE THE "OH WOW" MOMENTS?

_____

_____

_____

_____

_____

WHERE WERE THE SURPRISES?

_____

_____

_____

_____

_____

WHAT WERE THE POWERFUL WORDS YOU USED?

_____

_____

_____

_____

_____

_____

_____

WHAT DID YOU LIKE ABOUT THE SHOW?

_____

_____

_____

_____

_____

_____

_____

WHAT WAS MEMORABLE ABOUT THE SHOW?

_____

_____

_____

_____

_____

_____

_____

WHAT WORKED?

_____

_____

_____

_____

_____

_____

_____

WHAT COULD HAVE BEEN BETTER?

_____

_____

_____

_____

_____

_____

_____

_____

HOW DID YOU POSITION THE STORY FROM THE
LISTENER'S POINT OF VIEW?

_____

_____

_____

_____

_____

_____

_____

HOW DID YOU INCORPORATE THE LISTENER INTO THE
STORY TO MAKE THEM FEEL PART OF IT?

_____

_____

_____

_____

_____

_____

_____

WHERE DID YOU INTRODUCE THE SHOW/TOPIC?

WHERE DID YOU RESET THE SHOW/TOPIC?

_____

_____

_____

_____

_____

_____

HOW DID IT APPEAR YOU WERE PREPARED FOR EVERY

ELEMENT?

_____

_____

_____

_____

_____

_____

WHAT DID YOU REVEAL ABOUT YOURSELF TO HELP

FOSTER THE RELATIONSHIP WITH THE AUDIENCE?

_____

_____

_____

_____

_____

_____

WHAT STORIES DID YOU TELL?

_____

_____

_____

_____

_____

_____

_____

_____

WHAT DETAILS DID YOU USE THAT WERE SPECTACULAR
AND VISUAL?

_____

_____

_____

_____

_____

_____

_____

WHERE DID YOU USE ACTIVE LANGUAGE?   (WALKING
INSTEAD OF WALKED, EATING INSTEAD OF ATE)

_____

_____

_____

_____

_____

_____

WHAT CRUTCHES DO YOU USE THAT NEED TO BE REMOVED?

_____

_____

_____

_____

_____

_____

HOW CAN YOU MAKE TOMORROW BETTER?

_____

_____

_____

_____

_____

_____

_____

_____

_____

_____

_____

_____

_____

_____

_____

MONETIZATION

Most every podcaster has the desire to turn their podcast into a business. Though some podcasters treat their show as a hobby and an outlet for their passion, many reach a point where they wish to monetize their efforts. Podcast profits are possible in many forms when podcasters get creative.

Most podcasts do not generate enough cash to stand alone as a business. There are ways to generate revenue from the podcast, such as advertising and sponsorships. These methods typically bring in money in direct relation to the size of the audience. It is traditionally called CPM, or cost per thousand. (M being used as the Roman numeral for thousand.)

There are two primary issues with relying on advertising as your primary revenue source.

The first downside of CPM is the direct relation of hours to dollars.

When you stop putting in hours, you stop taking out dollars. When you stop creating the podcast, the revenue stream stops as well. When you exchange hours for dollars, that is called a job. When you create something one time and it generates a continuous stream of income, that becomes a business.

Limited inventory and revenue is the second problem with advertising. There is a limit to the amount of sponsorship time possible within any particular episode. If your podcast is an hour in length, how much advertising could the show possibly contain? Two sponsors? Four sponsors?

At some point, the advertising becomes a negative to the audience. This is the issue terrestrial radio is facing. The commercial time has expanded to a level that is negatively affecting time spent listening to radio. Stations are hoping listeners will sit through 12 minutes of commercials on music stations and nearly 20 minutes on talk stations. People are looking for other content that does not force feed them content they do not desire. This is where your podcast will thrive.

You can turn your podcast into a business by developing a suite of products. The podcast attracts a group of followers without wasting their time. Your content and message builds a friendships. Listeners begin to know, like and trust you.

Once you have built a loyal group of listeners that trusts you and your message, you can ask them to join your list in exchange for something free. This gets people to take the next step to become engaged with your brand. I use this with free worksheets, videos and other content. Fans give me permission to e-mail them pertinent, valuable content. The additional free content continues to build the relationship.

After delivering content over time, you can begin to monetize the trust you've built. Start by asking your fans to purchase a low end product, such as this workbook. The low end product doesn't cost much. It is simply a purchase to break the barrier to make your fan comfortable doing business with you. Your listener can risk $20 to see if your products are as good as you say. Again, we are building more trust.

If you could sell 1,000 e-books at $20 each to your audience of 10,000 listeners, you would generate $20,000 in revenue.

Let's compare that to the CPM model. The average CPM in podcasting is around $25. Using that same 10,000 listeners, your CPM factor would be ten, because you have ten "thousands". $25 CPM x ten "thousands" equals $250 per episode sponsorship. Two sponsors per episode would generate $500 per episode. Producing fifty episodes per year would then bring in $25,000 annually. That is just a little better than the e-book model.

There is a big difference between the two methods. With the e-book, you write it once. It then continues to generate revenue. You must create your podcast every week to keep the revenue flowing. At the beginning of the next year, your podcast starts over again. Your e-book continues to sell with little additional effort. You can also write another book to begin doubling your revenue.

The next step is a mid-range product. This would be something in the $200 range. While you continue to deliver great, free content and your book continues to sell and build trust, you can then produce your mid-level product. At some point, you will ask for that sale. Convincing 100 of your 10,000 fans to purchase your $200 product will generate $20,000. We are talking about converting one percent of your audience at this level.

This style of product layering continues as you build your business. It is all based on the relationships you are creating with your podcast. You are building trust with your podcast. The fantastic, free content allows your fans to know, like and trust you. Your podcast is the foundation of your business.

Your podcast is not your income generator. The relationships you have build with your audience becomes the conduit to create income. Your friendships will be the basis on which your business is built. We will turn those relationships into a suite of great products centered around your content.

"Entrepreneur on Fire" with John Lee Dumas is arguably one of the most successful recent podcasts in terms of revenue generation. John releases a daily podcast 365 days a year. He has been able to monetize his podcast at a high level using sponsorships. In fact, John posts his monthly income report on his website at www.EntrepreneurOnFire.com/income. According to his report, Dumas generated $39,400 from sponsorships in December 2013.

Even at that level of success, John Lee Dumas has other products. At nearly $40,000 a month, his show is bringing in almost half a million dollars in annual sponsorship revenue. If you examine the income report, advertising within the show isn't even the largest source of income during the month of December. Entrepreneur on Fire generated $52,763 with John's "Podcasters' Paradise" program.

In total, Dumas lists 7 different revenue sources on his income report. These include a mastermind, sponsorships, an ebook, an audiobook, his program, one-on-one mentoring and affiliates. This is a great example of a suite of products. The entire program is built on the foundation laid by his podcast.

If you hope to build a business around your podcast, begin by developing your product suite. Brainstorm the various products and services you can create. Make a list of five to ten products that will begin to generate revenue for you. Then, start creating the one that will be quick and easy. This is where your business will begin to take shape.

Your entire business will be built around your podcast. This is where people will begin to trust you. Everything described in this workbook up to this point has been designed to get your audience to know, like and trust you. Only when we reach that point can we begin to monetize the show.

You are creating a relationship with your audience. The more you reveal about yourself on your show, the more you create influence through friendship. Your sales will be built on the trust you are developing.

Help your audience. In sports coaching it is often said that players will not care how much the coach knows until they know how much the coach cares. Show your listeners you care by helping them solve their problems. Develop that friendship.

Once your friendship is built, your listeners will begin to move through your product funnel.

Your product funnel is just as it sounds. We bring many people into the big end of the funnel. As they move through, the price goes up until only a few come out the small end. Your podcast and other free content is at the big end of the funnel. As we move to the low-tier $20 product, we lose a group of listeners. We then lose another group when we progress to the $200 product. Listeners continue to move along the funnel until we have a few dedicated listeners playing thousands of dollars at the small end of the funnel.

You cannot begin at the middle of the funnel. People do not begin by buying your $200 without knowing anything about you. The entire funnel is based around your podcast and the relationships you are creating.

Though your podcast will not be your primary revenue generator, it will be the foundation for your business. This is where it all begins. Make it great. Tell the truth. Make it matter. Have fun. Before you know it, you will be building great friendships on the way to an amazing business.

CONCLUSION

Your income generator is your _relationship_ with your audience and the ways you leverage that relationship. It all begins by creating a very strong relationship. Your strong relationship begins with trust and takes time to develop.

You are now ready to use the four easy-to-understand steps to create winning podcasts. Find your passion. Create a solid strategy based on a target and structure. Fill your podcast with compelling, consistent content. Finally, be sure to review each podcast methodically to make the next one even better.

When you create a solid relationship with your audience, you have tremendous power. You can use that relationship to motivate your audience to action. That action could be support of your sponsor or partner, purchase of your product or attendance at an event. That motivation to action can generate income. It can generate large sums of income in a hurry, if you have first properly created the relationship.

I am always available to help you refine your podcast content. You can find me online at www.PodcastTalentCoach.com. Be exciting and have fun.

-Erik K. Johnson

<u>NOTES</u>

<u>NOTES</u>

<u>NOTES</u>